1   The Oxford photographer Henry W. Taunt (1842–1922) aboard his photographic boat in the 1890s. Many of the photographs in this book are his. He was also an antiquarian, musician, lecturer, writer, printer and publisher

2 Merton Street *c.*1857. The gabled building on the left where the carriage waits is St. Alban Hall, demolished 1905–7. Merton College beyond

Victorian and Edwardian

OXFORD

from old photographs

JOHN BETJEMAN
and
DAVID VAISEY

B T BATSFORD LTD

LONDON

B. T. Batsford Limited

4 Fitzhardinge St, London W1
Printed and bound in Great Britain by
Jarrold & Sons Limited, Norwich, Norfolk
First published 1971
7134 0118 4

CONTENTS

ACKNOWLEDGMENT

The authors are most grateful to the heads of houses, fellows, librarians, companies and individuals through whose kindness the photographs in this book were made available. In particular they wish to thank, for the pictures indicated: John Allen and Sons (Oxford) Limited, for Nos. 37, 38, 139. Sir John Betjeman, for Nos. 68, 69. The Bodleian Library for Nos. 2, 3, 4, 6, 10, 11, 12, 13, 14, 15, 16, 17, 18, 19, 20, 21, 22, 23, 25, 27, 28, 29, 30, 41, 42, 43, 48, 50, 55, 57, 58, 61, 63, 65, 66, 70, 78, 80, 81, 83, 96, 97, 103, 107, 108, 109, 120, 121, 122, 124, 128, 129, 130, 134, 136, 146, 147, 148, 151, 154, 156. Brasenose College Archives for Nos. 85, 94, 105. Brasenose College Senior Common Room for No. 92. British Leyland (Austin-Morris) Ltd., for Nos. 141, 142. P. J. Law, Esq., for No. 93. Mrs R. A. Crisp, Islip, for Nos. 110, 111, 112, 113, 114. The Crown Stores, Oxford, for No. 34. Mrs. M. Dring, Headington, for No. 144. A. R. Edney, Esq., Headington, for Nos. 143, 152. Exeter College Archives, for Nos. 137, 138, R. A. Gardner, Esq., Eynsham, for No. 132. Lady Margaret Hall, Senior Common Room, for Nos. 106, 149. J. H. R. Lynam, Esq., for Nos. 48, 52, 54. Magdalen College, for No. 119. Merton College Archives for Nos. 99, 100. Nuffield College Library, for No. 49. Oxford City Library, for Nos. 1, 5, 8, 24, 26, 31, 35, 36, 40, 45, 51, 53, 59, 75, 76, 77, 84, 87, 89, 90, 91, 98, 125, 126, 127, 131, 133, 135, 150. Oxford Union Society, for No. 79. Oxford University Museum, for Nos. 102, 116, 117, 118. Oxford University Press, for Nos. 56, 104. The Publishers, for Nos. 30, 33, 44, 46, 60, 62, 64, 101, 145, 153. Ruskin College Archives, for No. 95. Salter Brothers, Oxford, for Nos. 39, 123. St. Antony's College Library, for Nos. 71, 72. St. Edward's School, Oxford, for Nos. 47, 140. The Society of St. John the Evangelist, Oxford, for Nos. 73, 74. D. A. Tyler, Esq., Oxford, for Nos. 32, 115. The Warden of All Souls College, for Nos. 7, 9, 67, 82, 86, 88. The Controller, Wolvercote Paper Mill, for No. 155.

INTRODUCTION

After looking through the hundreds of old photographs of Oxford Mr. Vaisey had so thought-fully assembled, he and the publishers and I were exercised as to how to divide them. Unscathed like rocks in the seas of time, if I may use such trite grandiloquence, the towers and spires, college halls and chapels have survived from the middle ages. A late and lovely addition to the medieval cluster at the heart of the University, was eighteenth century. It was the Radcliffe Camera (1737–49) by James Gibbs, and it is still pre-eminent as it was in its contrasting cream and white stones when Gibbon was an undergraduate at Magdalen in 1752. The changes in the Oxford which tourists come to see have not, except for refacings of crumbling surfaces of mediaeval and Renaissance colleges, been particularly great. Miraculously too, Port Meadow, which belongs to the freemen of Oxford, and the village of Binsey with its streams and holy well and Wytham with its background of Berkshire woods, survive on the west. Christ Church meadow is still safe on the south, and the banks of the Cherwell from Magdalen Bridge to Summertown are much as they were when the poet Hurdis was a tassel'd student. Only the terrible intrusions of the Science Laboratories interfere with the famous skyline of City and University, these and a rather un-fortunate slab put up in St. Edmund Hall shock today's aesthete, as Butterfield's mighty Keble College shocked Oscar Wilde. Today's aesthete has more reason to be shocked, as the modern buildings have, with few exceptions, nothing like the distinction of Keble, which was built because brick was cheap and harmonised with the then new suburb of North Oxford.

> How changed is here each spot man makes or fills!
> In the two Hinkseys nothing keeps the same;
> The village-street its haunted mansion lacks,
> And from the sign is gone Sibylla's name,
> And from the roofs the twisted chimney-stacks;
> Are ye too changed, ye hills?

Indeed ye are changed, ye hills! So far as Oxford is concerned the change is largely due to the rather jaunty little man in the front of the Laurels Cycling Club group (Fig. 49) William R. Morris. As pioneer of the cheap motor car, the influence of his works at Cowley so encircled the Berkshire and Oxfordshire hills, which surround Oxford, that they are now acres of detached and semi-detached houses, blocks of flats and housing estates, gnomes, birdbaths and shopping arcades, by-passes and monster concrete floodlit highways leading to industrial estates. Little did this good and generous man who became Lord Nuffield know of the Frankenstein his industry would create. I have an idea it haunted his later years.

I first knew Oxford during World War I, when I came as a boy to what is variously known as the O.P.S., Lynam's or the Dragon School. I remember how pleasant it was to bicycle out into the country, when the Banbury Road was deserted, and how we used to make journeys through Park Town on foot to Ora Brown's sweetshop in North Parade, which was like a little village street – and still is. I remember gas-lit houses in North Oxford, and firework parties in their back gardens and tea parties on their leafy lawns, and strawberries and cream beside the muddy Cherwell

4   Rival boatbuilders on the Isis above Medley Weir, 1895. Port Meadow beyond

5   The head of the Oxford arm of the canal, 1900. Nuffield College now occupies the site

6 Magdalen Bridge shortly after its widening in 1890

where we used to swim. There were still hansoms in the streets and George Street looked like it does in Figure 18; the canal basin was a sight to see and I would go to tea in the Stone House, that Greek revival temple, where the Manager and his wife, Mr. and Mrs. Anderson lived. There were footpaths, along which we could bicycle to Marston Ferry through allotments. We could ride three abreast in elm-shaded lanes. The Oxford buses were worked by gas and had balloons on their top decks.

I was aware at this time of the difference and faint antagonism between Town and Gown. Town was definitely not thought so good as Gown. I had a great-uncle who was an architect in Oxford, but as he wasn't Sir Thomas Jackson or one of the architects who had been to the University, I remember him being referred to as a "townee". It mattered a lot in those days in hawthorn-scented North Oxford to which house in Norham Road, Crick Road or even as far out as Rawlinson Road, you were invited. Widows of Heads of Houses were Queens of North Oxford society. Polstead Road and Chalfont Road where I would go to tea, were slightly beyond the pale, and Summertown, except of course for Summerfields School, was out of the question. No one visited Cowley Road, except to hear plainsong in Bodley's beautiful church built for the Cowley Fathers, otherwise East Oxford was associated with commerce and those real bulwarks of the University, the college servants. To go to Jericho, now becoming fashionable as a residential place, was then

7, 8 May Morning. The choir on the top of Magdalen Tower, and the crowd on the bridge listening to their singing, 1895

to go slumming, though that was always permitted because it was "good work". The services at St. Barnabas with their ritual and incense, were a rival attraction to the Cowley Fathers. This has all been written from a North Oxford point of view.

When I came as an undergraduate to Oxford in 1925, the place had little changed. The round-nosed Morrises were much used by the lesser undergraduates like myself, and sports Bugattis and open Rollses by the richer. Bicycles were used by all classes and sexes.

It was while I was an undergraduate that I became aware that the town had a third quality besides Town and Gown, particularly on its western side in George Street and St. Ebbes and High Street St. Thomas's. This was the country town called Oxford to which farmers and their wives came on market days. There were seed shops and agricultural implement shops in St. Ebbes and George Street, and for people from Otmoor and beyond Headington and Shotover, there were similar shops in St. Clement's. St. Giles' Fair in September when the University was down was and still is the greatest gathering of Oxfordshire countrymen.

The University had its own shopping quarter and this was the Corn Market and the Carfax end of the High and the bookshops in the Broad. Secondhand bookshops abounded, and an undergraduate interested in English probably learned more from them than he did from his Tutor or from reading in the Bodleian. Dons were great characters as they still are, and became legendary figures in their lifetimes as they still do. Whatever the acidity in debates at college meetings about where to plant a new tree or how much to spend on the college cellar, death drew them together and they attended, as they still attend, memorial services. I rejoice in Belloc's Dedicatory Ode, (Belloc may be seen in Figure 101) because I like to think that these three stanzas are still true.

"Can this be Oxford? This the place?"
(He cries). "Of which my father said
The tutoring was a damned disgrace,
The Creed a mummery stuffed and dead?

Can it be here that Uncle Paul
Was driven by excessive gloom
To drink and debt, and, last of all
To smoking opium in his room?

Is it from here the people come,
Who talk so loud, and roll their eyes
And stammer? How extremely rum!
How curious! What a great surprise!"

People's characters whether they are town, gown or country, have changed less than their outer surroundings. That is why this book is more concerned to portray traffic, dress and ways of life, and some of the surrounding countryside. These have greatly changed.

John Betjeman

9   The lying-in-state of Mr. Thomas Combe (1872), a partner in the Oxford University Press, and donor of pre-Raphaelite pictures to the Ashmolean. He was a Tractarian and instrumental in building the Blomfield Byzantine church of St. Barnabas shewn here.

THE TOWN

10 High Street, south side, in August 1908, showing shops demolished, 1909–11 to make way for the Rhodes building by Basil Champneys

11   North side of the High Street in March 1887 before the introduction of electric
street lighting. The houses between Standen's the tailors on the corner and most of the
shops to the west of them were demolished soon after this picture to make way for the
Brasenose new building, 1897–1911, by Sir Thomas Jackson

12 Bird-in-Hand Passage or Swan Court. It joined the High Street with Bear Lane, and King Edward Street—a street constructed in 1871–5—is now on the site

13 The south side of the High Street before the construction of King Edward Street in 1871–5. The way in to Bird-in-Hand Passage was through the entrance to the right of the shop with the carved arms, on the left-hand side of the tallest building

14 Wheatsheaf Yard, south of the High Street, demolished 1896

15 The last of Oxford's sixteenth-century galleried inns was the old part of the King's Head Inn which the Clarendon had absorbed. Soon after this picture was taken in 1870 the inn was demolished, and the Clarendon Hotel was pulled down itself in 1954–5. Woolworths now occupies the whole site

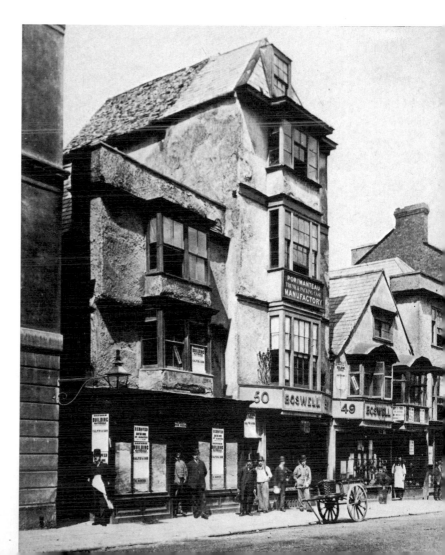

16 Boswell's shop at 49–50 Cornmarket c. 1870, just north of Frewin Court

17   The raised causeway (1661) and houses at the junction of George Street and Victoria Court where now the New Theatre stands, taken just before the demolition of the terrace in 1886. The door half way down led into an underground ice-house. The gabled building in the distance (Reid, printers) was demolished in 1935

18   The west end of George Street looking west up the street, 1870. None of these buildings now exists

19 The shop fronts facing the old New Theatre in George Street about 1900. Of these frontages only the late Victorian façade of The Grapes remains

20 New Inn Hall Street looking south, 1865, before the building of St. Peter's College. New Inn Hall (1832) is half way down on the right hand side

21 Cabs waiting outside the Taylorian Galleries in the 1880s. The Randolph Hotel, on the left, was built by William Wilkinson, 1864

22 "Seal's Coffee House." This Vanbrughesque building occupied the corner of Catte Street and Holywell Street where now stands the Indian Institute (Basil Champneys, 1889–95). Photograph, 1880

23 Looking up St. Aldate's to Carfax. On the right is the old Town Hall (1751, by Isaac Ware; demolished, 1892)

24 St. Aldate's from the south, *c.* 1910

25 *(Overleaf)* St. Aldate's looking north, 28th July 1904. The houses on the right have disappeared and the site is now occupied by Christ Church Memorial Gardens, Linacre College and the City Police Station

REPAIRS
NEATLY
EXECUTED

26 The Cape of Good Hope public house on the Plain at the junction of the Cowley and Iffley roads, 1892. The landlord and some of his staff at the door. The name remains but the building has been replaced

27 The Elm Tree public house at 95 Cowley Road on the corner of what is now Jeune Street, 1899

28   Shops on the east side of Walton Street at the junction with Little Clarendon Street just before demolition, *c.* 1890

29   The Horse and Jockey off the Woodstock Road, *c.*1870

30 Procession of elementary school children down Broad Street during the celebrations for Queen Victoria's jubilee, 28th June 1887; a photograph taken from a window in Henry W. Taunt's Broad Street Shop. The Indian Institute building does not yet fill the vista at the end of the Broad

THE LIFE OF THE TOWN

31   Avenue 2, covered market, 1909. Advertisements for ''Real Oxford Sausages'' refer to a particular sort of small sausage called Oxford Dainties for which the town was famed

32 A North Oxford butcher, Frederick Howard of 237a Banbury Road, Oxford, outside the shop where he began making his North Oxford sausages in 1913 (see also Fig. 115)

33 Until recent times the University and City have either been at war or on terms of uneasy peace over trading privileges. Up to 1889 the control of the covered market was vested in the Chancellor of the University. The University still appoints clerks of the market but the office is now purely formal. When this picture was taken in about 1909 the clerks still went to weigh the butter in the market. The clerk here is Dr. C. H. O. Daniel, Provost of Worcester (of Daniel Press fame) and the trader is Ernest Pigott at 21–24 the Market

34 The Crown Stores at 152 Cowley Road about 1907

35 Frank Cooper's Oxford Marmalade shop at 83 & 84 High Street at the end of the century. The shop is now closed and Oxford Marmalade is no longer a local product

36 Milkmen and their delivery trolleys outside the St. Aldate's dairy of Frank Wigmore, *c*.1910

37 A traction engine adapted for hauling ammunition wagons in the South African war by the Oxfordshire Steam Ploughing Company at Cowley (now John Allen & Sons (Oxford) Ltd.), *c.* 1900

38 Part of the boiler shop, *c.*1908

39 Boatbuilders in Salter Bros'. workshop about 1905. The man with the bow tie was the foreman-boatbuilder, Baker. It was a mark of a good boat that she was called "Baker-built".

40 The cattle market on Gloucester Green in the 1890s. The market moved from here in 1931, and it is now the bus station. The row of old houses on the right was demolished before 1900 when the handsome school, by Leonard Stokes, now the bus office was built on the site

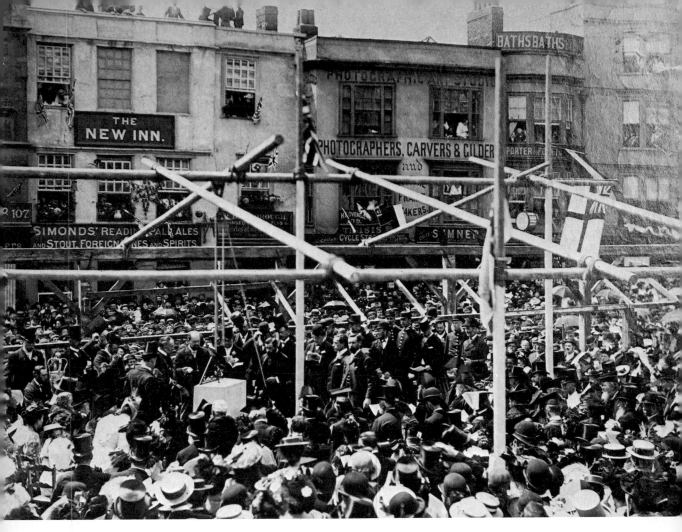

41 Alderman Thomas Lucas, mayor of Oxford, laying the foundation stone of the new Town Hall in St. Aldate's, 6th July 1893. The architect was Henry T. Hare

42 The Oxfordshire Militia on parade in the garden of St. John's College in the early 1860s.

43 The Oxford Rifle Volunteers marching to the G.W.R. railway station, setting out for camp at Aldershot on 11th August 1883. The London and North Western Railway terminus (now a car-tyre depot) is on the left

44   Jubilee ox-roast at Osney, 21st June 1887

45   The Oxford sweeps' May Day procession outside Balliol College, 1886, with a "Jack in the Green"; a "Lord and Lady" (both in fact male) dressed in white and carrying a ladle and a frying pan; a "fool" carrying a bladder; a fiddler; two or three men with money boxes; and a man with a shovel and poker for making a noise

46 Beating the bounds of the parish on Ascension Day. Choristers and parish officials of St. Mary the Virgin

47 An informal group of St. Edward's school boys in 1875. The Headmaster (later Warden) was A. B. Simeon

48   A group of tennis players at the pavilion in the University Parks, *c*.1900

49   The Laurels Cycling Club on its annual boating party in 1900. The leading member of the club—in the white boots at the front—is William R. Morris, later to become Lord Nuffield

FAIRS

50   An open-air theatrical performance at St. Giles Fair, *c.*1865; photograph by Richard
Phené Spiers

51   *(overleaf)* St. Giles Fair: A roundabout, "fare 1d", *c.* 1905

FARE
1

52   St. Giles Fair: the swings

53 St. Giles Fair: the Bible stall, 1895

54 St. Giles Fair, when Oxfordshire comes to Oxford and the University sinks into the background

55   Stalls in the long-vanished St. Clements Fair, *c.*1906

FIRE, FLOODS AND STORMS

56   The Oxford University Press Volunteer Fire Brigade, 1898

57 *(opposite)* The aftermath of the fire at Grimbly, Hughes & Dewe, grocers, in Corn-market Street during the night of 20th September 1863. Seven private fire crews attended (including the University, the Clarendon Hotel and Morrell's Brewery) but it was half an hour before the water could be switched on and then many of the appliances would not work. The direct result of this blaze and of another in St. Aldate's soon afterwards was the formation of the Volunteer Fire Brigade. The shop was rebuilt in Venetian Gothic by William Wilkinson in 1864

58 An inspection parade of the Oxford Volunteer Fire Brigade in Broad Street, c.1890

59 Ice-hockey being played on the flooded and frozen Christ Church meadows, *c.*1895

60 A coach and six on the frozen river, 16th February 1895. In the background are the now-vanished college barges; from right to left, those of Oriel (with round windows), Christ Church, University, Exeter, Brasenose, and the university barge

61 The approach to the G.W.R. railway station in the great flood of 1875. The flood was caused by the Isis breaking its banks on Sunday, 14th November. Under the Botley Road bridge the water was 9–10 feet deep. Passengers were conveyed to the station in punts

62 An Oxford Tramways Company horse bus (*left*) with other traffic stopped in floods on the Cowley Road, *c.* 1902

CHURCHES

63 The Cornmarket, c. 1864, from the tower of St. Michael at the Northgate to that of St. Mary Magdalene

64 St. Martin's Church at Carfax from the High Street before its demolition in 1896.
With the exception of the tower it had been completely rebuilt to designs by John
Plowman of Oxford in 1820–22 and was the city church

65 The evangelical interior of St. Martin's. The East window was transferred to St. Clement's church

66 St. Peter le Bailey old church, rebuilt in 1740 and pulled down in 1874 for road widening

67 St. Mary the Virgin. The spire was restored in 1861 by J. C. Buckler. It was later found that the pinnacles and the statues at the base were in a dangerous condition and a later reconstruction was carried out by Sir Thomas Jackson, 1892–6

68 SS. Philip and James, by G. E. Street, 1860-6

69 SS. Philip and James: the interior as it used to be

70 *(overleaf)* The Cornmarket looking north in the 1890s. Behind the leading horses' head on the right was the entrance to the Blue Anchor Inn, one of the old country carrier's inns

71, 72 The old and new chapels of the Holy Trinity Convent (now St. Antony's College) in Woodstock Road. The new chapel superseded the old in 1894: it was designed by J. L. Pearson

73 The Iron Church – the first church of the parish of Cowley St. John – built by Father R. M. Benson in 1859

74 The Rev. Richard Meux Benson, the Vicar of Cowley and later of Cowley St. John, who in 1866 founded the Society of St. John the Evangelist (the Cowley Fathers). He is seated in the centre of a group of his parishioners outside the Iron Church – the first church of Cowley St. John – which was built in 1859 in Stockmore Street

GOWN

76 Two of Oxford's most eminent Victorians: (left) Sir Henry Acland, Regius Professor of Medicine, and (centre) Benjamin Jowett, Master of Balliol, outside the Master's lodgings; the bearded gentleman is W. W. Merry, Rector of Lincoln College

75 *(opposite)* Turl Street outside Lincoln College, *c.*1881

77 New College Lane seen from the Sheldonian Theatre in the 1880s, before Sir Thomas Jackson extended Hertford College and built the Bridge of Sighs

79 The old smoking room at the Oxford Union as re-decorated 1909–10

80 The Upper Reading Room of the Old Bodleian Library in 1907, when the north-east wing was still used as a picture gallery. Le Sueur's statue, visible at the end of the gallery, of the Earl of Pembroke now stands in the Bodleian quadrangle

81 Magdalen tower and the bridge before it was widened, *c.*1865

82 Christ Church from Carfax tower, 1864, before Bodley and Garner's tower was built (1879) at the east end of the Christ Church hall

83 Broad Street frontage of Balliol College, demolished in 1867

84 The Dolphin Building to the south of St. John's College in St. Giles. It was once an inn and has now been demolished

85 Undergraduates and a college cook outside staircase 9 in Brasenose College, back quadrangle (1886). The building stood behind Nos. 27–29 High Street and was demolished in 1909

86 Worcester College: Sharpe's rooms, 1897 (formerly Aston's 1893–5).

87   The first chapel at Keble College. Used from 1870 until 1876 when the present enormous chapel was built by Butterfield

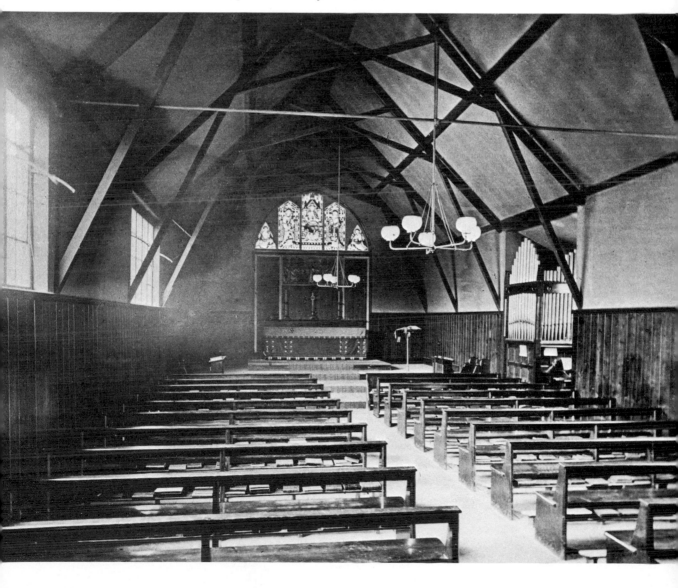

88 Worcester College: the Hall, finished in 1784, as redecorated by William Burges, 1877, who designed the fireplace

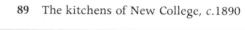

UNIVERSITY EVENTS

91   The procession to Encaenia passing Brasenose College, 22nd June, 1904. Viscount Goschen, the recently installed chancellor of the University leads

92   Their Royal Highnesses the Prince and Princess of Wales presenting prizes to the Oxford University Volunteer rifle corps on 16th June, 1863, in Tom Quad, Christ Church

93 The cast of the Oxford University Dramatic Society's production of *The Merry Wives of Windsor* at the New Theatre in February, 1896. Ann Page was played by Lillian Braithwaite

94   The marquee erected for Commemoration Ball at Brasenose College, 1887

95   The students of Ruskin College, who went on strike in 1909, shown moving out of the college

PERSONALITIES

96 A photograph taken in 1893 by Miss Sarah A. Acland of her father, Sir Henry Acland *(right)* with John Ruskin

97   Albert Edward, Prince of Wales, aged 18, with a cricket team during Commemoration Week, 1860

98   Charles Cox, proprietor of Parson's Pleasure, the bathing place for gentlemen, photographed in 1913 at the age of 88. He had worked at the bathing place since 1838

99 The Warden of Merton College and some of the fellows, 1877. R. H. B. Marsham was Warden from 1826 to 1880 when he died at the age of 94 and was succeeded by C. C. Brodrick who sits on his left. Seated on the ground, left, is F. H. Bradley, the philosopher

100 The Oxford Boat Race Crew of 1866. The race, rowed on 24th March, 1866, was won for the sixth time in succession by Oxford

101   The committee of the Union in 1895. The middle row, from left to right, shows John Bradbury, F. E. Smith, J. K. Macdonell, Hilaire Belloc, J. A. Simon

102   A photograph taken by C. L. Dodgson (Lewis Carroll) in 1858 of four Oxford scientists

103 The 'Old Mortality', a group of undergraduates who met in the rooms of John Nichol at Balliol. In this photograph taken in 1860 are: *(seated, left to right)* G. R. Luke, A. C. Swinburne, Nichol, A. V. Dicey, T. E. Holland; *(standing, left to right)* J. F. Payne, J. W. Hoole, T. H. Green, J. Bryce, A. J. G. Mackay

104   The Oxford University Press Band, *c*.1884

105   A group of Brasenose College servants in 1861

106 The young ladies of Lady Margaret Hall (founded 1878) photographed in Hilary Term, 1888. Seated in the centre is Miss (later Dame) Elizabeth Wordsworth, the Hall's first principal. Sideways on to the camera in that row is Gertrude Bell.

EVERYDAY LIFE

107   The Spiers children playing "lawn billiards", and "hunt the slipper" in the garden in July, 1857

108 Business family. Richard James Spiers, F.S.A., J.P., with his family in the garden of their house at 14 St. Giles, 1856. His son, Richard Phené Spiers, later to become an authority on architecture and the photographer of some of the pictures in this book, is third from the left.

109 *(overleaf)* Herbert Wilson Greene, M.A., B.C.L., fellow and vice-president of Magdalen College in his rooms in Magdalen College New Building, 12th May, 1903

110–114 The family of James Walker M.A., of Christ Church, lived in the North Oxford suburb of Norham Gardens

111 *(opposite)* Mrs. Walker in her drawing room, 30 Norham Gardens, 1904

110 The nanny, Eliza Bly, 1904

113 Three Walker children, *c.* 1899

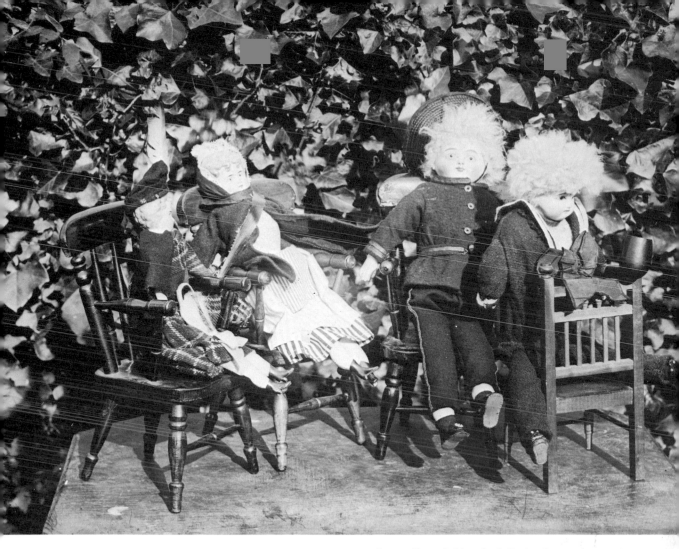

114   The Walker children's dolls in the garden, *c*.1899

115 A North Oxford butcher, Frederick Howard, of 273a Banbury Road, Oxford, picnicking with his family beside the Cherwell, *c.* 1908 (see also Fig. 32)

THE MUSEUM

116   The University Museum in course of erection, 1859–61. It was designed by Benjamin
Woodward, and structurally complete in 1860 but not finished internally for some years
afterwards. Much of the labour was performed by Irishmen brought over from Dublin by
Woodward, and in the "barracks", visible here, a rest room and reading room were
provided for them; books were supplied and lectures and morning prayers held there.
The building, which then stood in splendid isolation, is now completely hemmed in by
laboratories

117   One of the O'Shea brothers carving.

But if you allow them to vary their designs, and thus interest their heads and hearts in what they are doing, you will find them eager first, to get their ideas expressed, and then to finish the expression of them; and the moral energy thus brought to bear on the matter quickens, and therefore cheapens, the production in a most important degree. Sir Thomas Deane, the architect of the new Museum at Oxford, told me, as I passed through Oxford on my way here, that he found that, owing to this cause alone, capitals of various design could be executed cheaper than capitals of similar design (the amount of hand labour in each being the same) by about 30 per cent.
          – John Ruskin, *A Joy for Ever*, 1857

119 A waterman on the Thames, 1859, down river from Folly Bridge

THE RIVER AND THE CANAL

120   A scene on the river during Eights Week, 1889, with a paddle-steamer easing its way between punts and canoes

121   Trinity College barge with the college eight alongside it in 1889

122   The procession past the barges during Eights Week, 1889

123 A river steamer at Salters under the supervision of Baker (see Fig. 39) in 1905. The steamer was built for the Baptist Missionary Society for use in the Belgian Congo

124 The premises of J. & S. Salter at Folly Bridge, c.1860. On the left is the old lock on the navigable branch of the river at the bridge

125 The launching ceremony of the lifeboat *Isis*, 1866, at Folly Bridge

126 Abel Beesley on his punt on the river between Hythe Bridge and Pacey's Bridge in the 1890s. Beesley was for many years champion professional punter on the Thames

ABEL BEESLEY
University.
WATERMAN
Fish & Baits
Sold Here

127 The coal yard of Frank Restall on the Oxford Canal at Hayfield Wharf at the end of the century

128 (overleaf) Fisher Row looking south from Hythe Bridge, c.1900. The Row was destroyed c.1930

129   The Floating Chapel at Hythe Bridge opened in 1839 for the use of the barge population on river and canal, which run parallel at this point. Services were held there and it acted as a school for the children. It was removed in 1872

130   Hythe Bridge, c.1860, before its demolition ten years later

131   Navvies making the new cut for the Cherwell through Christ Church Meadow, 1883

ROADS AND TRANSPORT

132   An Oxford Tramways Company horse bus at Iffley Turn, *c*.1910

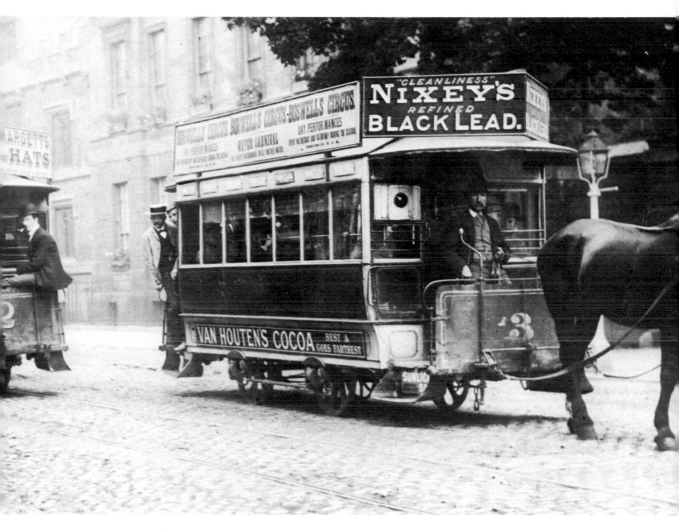

133   An Oxford Tramways Company horse tram in the High, *c.*1890. These trams ran from 1881 to 1913 when motor buses superseded them

134   The toll gate on the Plain at the East end of Magdalen Bridge, *c.*1868

135   Workmen replacing kidney stones in front of the shop of Henry W. Taunt, the photographer, at 9–10 Broad Street, 1881

136 Workers on the "Ruskin Road" to Ferry Hinksey, 1874. This project was devised by John Ruskin to demonstrate the dignity of labour and to employ the energies of undergraduates more usefully than in athletics. It resulted in an unfinished, indifferent road. When enthusiasm had died, the surveyor sent by the landowner reported on the project "the young men have done no mischief to speak of". The gang with which Ruskin himself worked on occasion as a stone-breaker, included, at various times, Arnold Toynbee, Oscar Wilde, Andrew Lang and Alfred Milner.

Thus, when I had to direct road making at Oxford, I sate, myself, with an iron-masked stone-breaker, on his heap, to break stones beside the London road, just under Iffley Hill, till I knew how to advise my too impetuous pupils to effect their purpose in that matter, instead of breaking the heads of the hammers off (a serious item in our daily expenses).

–John Ruskin, *Praeterita*, 1889

137   The Exeter College Coach and Four outside the college, 1909, on their way to the
"grind" (college steeplechase)

138   The Exeter College conveyance of 1910, a new Renault car

139 Mrs. John Allen, one of the first lady drivers in Oxford at the wheel of her Daimler, 1900

140 A group of cyclists at the lodge of St. Edward's school, 9th July, 1897

141 W. R. Morris' garage in Longwall Street with the hire-cars lined up outside, *c.*1907. Morris was not at this time building his own cars (his first car was produced in 1913), but by this date had given up making and repairing motor cycles to concentrate on hiring and repairing motor cars. As can be seen here the word MOTOR has been blacked out before CYCLE on the hoarding. Morris himself is seated in the passenger seat of the car on the far right

142 A coach and four outside W. R. Morris' first showrooms at 48 High Street, opposite the Examination Schools, c.1902. Morris occupied these premises from 1900 to 1908

THE SUBURBS AND THE COUNTRY

143 The Headington Quarry Sheep-roast, 1899. Seated with legs crossed and with the umbrella is G. Herbert Morrell, of Headington Hill Hall, whose brewery provided beer for the occasion

144   A Sunday school outing setting off in Old High Street, Headington, *c*.1910. Holding the reins in the leading wagonette is Alfred Dring, the carrier of Headington, whose conveyance (called The Rocket) ran a passenger service between Headington and the centre of Oxford

145   The Headington Quarry Morris Dancers outside the Chequers at Headington Quarry, 1898

146   The Woodstock Road looking North from near the corner of Staverton Road, taken on June 1st, 1903. The last remains of the grassy strip which had run the whole length of the road on its East side is on the right

147 At the north end of Kingston Road, 1872. The house is the Anchor Inn and the lane beyond is now Hayfield Road

148 *(overleaf)* A team of horses hauling timber at Godstow during the felling of trees preparatory to widening the river, 1885. The bearded man standing on the bank above the leading horse is probably the photographer, Henry W. Taunt

149 Three young ladies of Lady Margaret Hall on the river with the Hall in the background (*c*.1896)

150 A barge belonging to William Ward and Co., coal, coke and slate merchants on the Oxford Canal just north of Hythe Bridge in the 1890s

151 Looking north up the canal in the late 1860s. The brick bridge in the distance is that where Aristotle Lane now crosses the canal, and the rising ground to the right over the lifting bridge is where Southmoor Road and the northern end of Kingston Road are now

152 The sheep-dip at Bayswater Brook about 1900. This is now the Barton Estate

154 Jacob Beesley's osier yard just up river from Hythe Bridge, *c.*1874. Beesley stands on the right with the finished eel-traps and crayfish creels. The workers are mainly engaged in peeling osiers

155 Workers from the Wolvercote paper mill during hay-making in the 1880s. On the left stands the Controller of the mill from 1883 to 1916, Joseph Castle. The women were rag-pickers at the mill.

156 For long the first and last view of Oxford for the visitor coming from London by train: the gasworks in St. Ebbes, while it was being built in the early 1880s. It is now demolished